The Miracle of Matthew: God's Child

KATHY K. SURRATT

Copyright @ 2018 by Kathy K. Surratt All Rights Reserved
Printed in the United States of America
International Standard Book Number:
978-1-5323-6865-3

Kathy K. Surratt
Chandler, Texas
Email: kksurratt@yahoo.com

Co-authored:
Our Lord and Savior, Jesus Christ Kathy K. Surratt
Matthew Gilbert

Scripture quotations marked (NIV) are taken from the HOLY BIBLE, NEW INTERNATIONAL VERSION®. NIV®. Copyright © 1973, 1978, 1984 by International Bible Society. Used by permission of Zondervan. All rights reserved.

No part of this book may be reproduced or transmitted in any form or by any means, electronic or mechanical including photocopying, recording, or by any information storage and retrieval system, without permission in writing from Little Sparrow Ministries.

INGRAM BOOK DISTRIBUTOR

INTRODUCTION

The name Matthew means "God's child." Matthew is my nephew, my husband's sister's son. God revealed Himself in such a powerful way to our family that we wanted to share the events that took place and record them in the pages of this book.

I dedicate this book to parents who face overwhelming odds and have come face-to-face with the heartbreaking fact that their child is physically or mentally handicapped. My purpose is to share with, encourage, and give hope to those parents or anyone who find themselves in a seemingly hopeless situation.

May God turn your hopelessness into the joy that comes from hoping in Him!

Kathy K. Surratt

TABLE OF CONTENTS

Chapter One 1
Doctor's prognosis rocks our world!

Chapter Two 13
God speaks in amazing ways!

Chapter Three 29
We study, and God encourages!

Chapter Four 35
God shows up and shows off!

Chapter Five................................. 51
God offers hope to the hopeless!

Chapter Six 61
The parents' perspective!

Chapter Seven.............................. 69
Consumed by the Word of God!

Postscript 79
Matthew Gilbert

Epilogue..83
    Kathy K. Surratt

CHAPTER ONE
Doctor's prognosis rocks our world!

The telephone ring interrupted the intense Boggle game in which my husband and I were playing with some friends of ours. The clock displayed eleven p.m. I commented, preoccupied with the game, "Wonder who that could be?" It was my sister-in-law. Her voice sounded strained and on the verge of tears.

"Kathy, I want you to pray for us." In our eleven years of marriage, my sister-in-law had never asked for prayer; so, I knew that this must be something serious.

She went on to explain, "Something is wrong with Matthew's eyes. We took him to the doctor today, but he didn't like what he saw. He has made an appointment for us with a pediatric ophthalmologist in Shreveport tomorrow."

"Well," I replied slowly, "What does the doctor think is wrong?"

"I don't know," she said. "But Matt has an eye movement that he called "nystagmus," and this indicates that there is an eye problem that needs further study."

I promised to pray with the thought that maybe Kathy was over-reacting to her newborn, and I returned to our game. I did pray, but I never felt any real concern that there would be anything seriously wrong. After all, the baby was just six weeks old. I thought a baby's eyesight wasn't very clear at that age; so, probably we had nothing to worry about.

The next day, while busy with housework, I would stop and think about Kathy, her husband, Dennis, and the baby. Late that afternoon the phone rang, and the near hysterical voice on the other end of the line revealed my mother-in-law, Dorothy. She called to tell me that things were indeed serious.

The doctor said that Matthew had serious developmental problems with his eyes. In fact, the harsh, un-cushioned words of the doctor had been, "Matthew is BLIND. There is nothing anyone can do." As my mind raced to absorb the reality of those words, I was flooded with a feeling of frustration over the hopelessness of the prognosis.

"Are you sure? What did the doctor say? What is the next step?" I stammered as my mind reeled from the news.

Dorothy said, "Kathy, can you come up here? Kathy and Dennis are devastated, and no one can seem to talk to Kathy. Maybe she will listen to you."

I couldn't seem to find any words to say except that I would come and do what I could. I asked to speak to Kathy, not knowing what to say. "You got your feet knocked out from under you today, huh, girl?" I said softly. She began to cry; and I continued,

"Kathy, God is greater than any doctor, and He always has the final word, not the doctors. Do you want me to come?" She said that she would like that. I prayed with her and hung up. Fear gripped my heart over the disturbing news I had just heard; but I didn't have time to dwell on it, because I had plans to make. I lived four hours from Kathy and Dennis, and I wanted to get there as soon as possible.

I literally threw some things in a suitcase. I then interrupted my husband-coach's basketball practice to fill him in on what was going on with his sister. I then got our kids settled and left on the long drive from Huntsville to Linden, Texas.

As I drove, the fear began to creep back into my mind. I started to think about what I could say to comfort Kathy and Dennis. I had always shared with people I met about the healing power of God, but I had never talked about anything this serious. This involved my family.

Sure, God can do anything. I knew that, but would He heal a baby who is blind? The word "blind" sounds so permanent, so final. Does God still heal the blind like He did in biblical times? It proved to be a faith-testing time for me as well as our family. I felt very sure that the Lord wanted me to go and share what I knew about the love and healing power of God with Kathy and Dennis. I also felt inadequate for the tasks ahead. I realized later that I had been prepared as much as one could be for a crisis such as this.

I was born into a family that had taught me to have a strong faith in God. My dad, a Methodist minister, and my mother had taught me in many ways about how man's extremities become God's opportunities.

As an adult, I had experienced, firsthand, a few times when doctors had said that nothing could be done for me only to watch God perform the impossible. The seeds had been planted in me to not accept "impossible" as a final word on any situation. With this personal knowledge as a backdrop, and my personal studies in the Bible on physical healing as a foundation, I found myself very sure that God's healing power was for Matt.

As the miles wore on, I prayed, thought, and reflected on all the miracles that I had witnessed during my lifetime. I remembered all the wonderful, exciting answers to prayer, and my faith began to rise. I felt excited about what God was going to do.

As a rude intruder, though, one thought kept interrupting all the positive thoughts. "What if you hold out false hope to Kathy and Dennis? What a horrible thing to do. What will people say? What will Gary's family say?" As I mulled these questions over in my mind, like a ray of sun peeping through gray skies, the thought developed: "But hope is never false when it is in the Lord!" We were forced to remind ourselves of this thought many times throughout the months to come.

CHAPTER TWO
God speaks in amazing ways!

When I arrived in Linden that night, the atmosphere in the house resembled that of a funeral home where families gather to share their grief and shock over having lost a loved one. Everyone, except for Dude, my father-in-law, seemed extremely depressed, and a feeling of hopelessness permeated the house.

The devastation the family felt over the doctor's words was overwhelming, and as I entered this scene I wasn't sure what to do. I began to talk to each member of the family one at a time to try to plant some seeds of hope. Kathy experienced so much pain that she couldn't even hold the baby; so, his needs became important for me to meet as no one in the family could concentrate on even the smallest of chores.

The next morning, with little sleep for anyone, I entered the living room to find Dennis in the rocking chair, rocking and crying. As I approached him, my heart broke to see the hurt I knew he was experiencing. I knelt beside him and said, "Dennis, God can heal your baby."

"Dennis replied sadly, distantly, "I know He can, but will he heal my baby?" "Yes, I believe He will," I declared.

We prayed and cried and talked as we prepared to go to Dallas that morning to take Matt to another doctor for a second opinion. The doctor in Shreveport had reluctantly made this appointment for Kathy and Dennis when they became so distraught. He bluntly advised them to, "Just take the child home and love it."

When Dennis asked if there was anywhere in the world they could take Matt and get some help for him, the doctor was trying to be honest and forthright about the facts, but these were cruel words to two young parents who desperately needed to be encouraged. They needed time to adjust to the bad news. In the doctor's report he noted that because the parents had become so distraught, he would send them to another doctor for the second opinion.

By the time we got in the car to leave for Dallas, everyone had calmed down somewhat. We started on our way to pick up Dorothy and had only traveled a short way when Kathy began to cry. I thought, "Oh, no, just when I thought we had all calmed down!" This time, though, her cry expressed joy! While reading her Bible, she randomly opened it, and her eyes fell on Psalm 146:8:

"The Lord gives sight to the blind, the Lord lifts up those who are bowed down, the Lord loves the righteous."

God was beginning to speak, and for the next two days he certainly did speak to us. God is a speaking God. He longs to speak to His children; but, many of us only open our ears to listen and hear when we find our backs against the wall and when our needs can be met in Him and Him alone.

When we arrived at Dorothy's house, her pastor was waiting. We had prayer together and continued on our way.

We arrived in Dallas, and Kathy didn't want to go in with Matt to see the doctor; so, Dennis and I took him in. Dennis had prayed before we entered the office that the Lord would give us some sign, any sign of encouragement. The doctor seemed very kind, and although non-committal, stated that Matt's eye problem appeared extremely serious, but that we always hope things can change.

His words were just a minute bit of encouragement, but Dennis didn't need any more. He ran to get Kathy, so she could hear for herself what the doctor said. I'll always believe that this doctor was a Christian, and he sensed the desperate need of this young couple to know of a higher power beyond that of medical science.

The doctor told Kathy that Matt's problems fell somewhere between blind and 2O/2O vision.

He said that Matt was too young to know the exact future outcome; but, that he did have atrophy of the optic nerve which means an undeveloped optic nerve and an unchangeable condition.

As we entered the elevator to leave the building, Dennis and I talked excitedly about the doctor's cautious, but hopeful words. Dennis's prayer had been answered. Kathy remained more skeptical and adopted a "wait and see" attitude. Dennis, on the other hand, intended to witness to his excitement. He exuberantly announced to an unsuspecting lady who was riding the elevator with us that God surely was good and could do anything! As one might imagine, she appeared slightly nervous and didn't have much to say. In fact, she exited that elevator as quickly as she had the opportunity to do so. We laughed about our reluctant, captive lady who clearly did not share our enthusiasm!

At the request of the doctor, we went to another hospital in Dallas to see a pediatric neurologist. The hospital stood imposingly, and we felt in awe of both the hospital and the doctor.

He examined Matt, did some tests, and later came in to see us. He bluntly, pointedly stated, "Your baby is blind. He may see a small shadow of light, but nothing more. He has an undeveloped optic nerve for which there is no cure. He may go to school someday, but to a school for the blind."

Stunned by the doctor's diagnosis and prognosis, we felt as if we had been slapped in the face, unable to defend ourselves. We asked every question possible, frantically searching for some ray of hope. He gave none. We all left that office despondent, and for the first time, I felt like we had approached a wall too big to climb over. "After all," I thought, "these doctors represent the best in their fields. They know their business, and they leave no room for answers beyond what they know to be fact. Maybe it is crazy to believe that God will heal Matt."

Slowly, Kathy and Dennis walked out of the hospital ahead of Dorothy and me. We carried the baby. Discouraged, we felt the dark cloud of fear hovering over us.

Absorbed in our thoughts, we became aware of someone

singing behind us quite a distance down the hall. We talked quietly, not paying attention to the voice that got closer and closer. I felt slightly annoyed that he was interrupting our conversation. However, as the man passed us we stopped talking and heard him singing these words: "I thank you, Father, that you open the eyes of the blind." His words startled us, and we looked at each other. Then we looked in the direction of the voice. What we saw amazed us, and we stared in disbelief as we witnessed an elderly, African-American man in a tan trench coat and an old fishing-type hat. He held a Bible in one hand, raised in the air, and shuffled past us not in a hurry. He continued singing; his eyes focused ahead, and he was seemingly oblivious to us. As he passed, Dorothy and I stopped right in the middle of the hall staring at each other in astonishment. We were approaching the turning point to exit the hallway. We turned to look at him again, and he was gone. Whether he went into a room or down another hall we weren't sure; he simply vanished from sight. We were left speechless and overwhelmed by what we had just witnessed. He had sung the words that Kathy read in the Bible that morning!

Finally, I said, "I think that man may have been an angel!!! When we gathered our senses, we hurried to the car to tell Kathy and Dennis what had happened.

Our faith was strengthened and encouraged. We knew that God had spoken again and was encouraging us to hope in Him. The "coincidence" of being in a large, city hospital with a blind baby in our arms and having a man pass us singing about how

God opens the eyes of the blind seemed too much to be coincidence. It sounded more like a "God-incidence" to me.

CHAPTER THREE
We study, and God encourages!

The next day Kathy, Dennis, and I spent the day in the Bible. I shared every scripture I knew about physical healing. This subject is not very relevant to us until we have a need in our lives. Amazingly, the Bible has a lot to say about this subject. They were eager hearers and anxious to learn everything they could about this good news.

A genuine change emerged in them as they planted God's Word in their hearts and placed their trust in Him. The doctors had said all that they could say; now we needed to listen to what God had to say. We shared, cried, prayed, and studied. I made a list of scriptures for them and encouraged them to stand on those scriptures. This session around the dining room table lasted all day. Finally, at 9:00 p.m., I left for Tyler where I had taken one of my kids to stay. As I was leaving, Dorothy told me to call Kathy and Dennis every day and talk to them as long as there was a need. I promised I would and left.

In the car as I drove to Tyler, physically I felt exhausted, but spiritually I had never experienced such exhilaration. The presence of the Lord filled my car, and I worshipped Him as I never had before. I was keenly aware that I had been allowed to be a part of something God was doing. What a blessing!

This humbled me to know that maybe I had "...come into the kingdom for such a time as this." There is no greater joy in life than to know one has been used to serve God. If this point in time was the reason for which I was born, then serving God made my life fulfilling and worthwhile.

I arrived in Tyler very late. About midnight the phone rang. The voice on the other end revealed Kathy calling to tell me about something that had happened to her. She had been debating about how to pray for Matt, and she was questioning about whether to pray for some vision, good vision, or perfect vision.

She absentmindedly picked up an old newspaper, and her eyes fell to the Ann Landers section of the paper. The first article was entitled, "20/20 Hindsight." Excitedly, she once again felt God speaking to her situation through an unlikely "coincidence." The Lord was so faithful to encourage each of us every step of the way on our journey of faith in Him.

CHAPTER FOUR
God shows up and shows off!

As time went on, Kathy and I spent many hours on the phone with each other. We shared scriptures and encouraged each other. Each time I heard a testimony of how the Lord had moved in the life of someone, I would call her and tell her about it. "The 700 Club," a television program, provided many opportunities to share with her about personal testimonies of dramatic healings that other "ordinary" people had experienced.

Another doctor, this time in Houston, was recommended to Kathy and Dennis. They decided to continue to get opinions by the best pediatric ophthalmologists they could find. In February, we traveled to Houston to see a doctor who also gave us no hope for Matt. In fact, two specialists agreed that Matt was born with the same condition, bilateral hypoplasia of the optic nerve. He also had a nystagmus which caused a pronounced, involuntary eye movement visible to anyone.

Again, the doctor's bluntness stung us and gave little hope. On the way home from hearing the discouraging news, I opened the Bible and began to read the first chapter of 1st Corinthians about how God had chosen the weak things of this earth to put to shame the things that are mighty. I thought, "What could be weaker than a baby?" This scripture gave us the knowledge that God would get the glory from our situation.

The next day we had another appointment with a different pediatric ophthalmologist.

On the way to Houston, we listened to a tape that inspired us to pray in a different way than we had before. In the parking lot before we went in, we prayed that Satan would take his hands off this child's eyes. Satan, the tape reminded us, remains our enemy and intends to kill, steal, and destroy the perfect things of God. He robs God's children of the good gifts God has prepared for them.

As we entered the office, the doctor looked at us a little skeptically as mother, father, and aunt walked in with the baby. She muttered something about bringing the whole family to which I inwardly smiled. We had experienced a lot together, and we wanted to hear everything that was said about Matt-together.

Dr. Helen Hitner spent quite a long time with Matt and then said, "l have some good news and some bad news. He is far from blind. There is absolutely nothing wrong with his optic nerve; it is as good as mine. He does have an ocular albinism which is a lack of pigment behind the eye. Also, he has an under-developed macula, which is the focal point where images are made sharp."

We thought she had made some mistake in her understanding of Matt's problem because we had not told her about the other doctors or their reports.

We began to vigorously question her about the optic nerve and all the other things we had been told about his problems. We really badgered the poor doctor, and we finally pulled out the other doctors' reports that said just the opposite of what she had just told us. She reviewed the reports very carefully. She then folded them up and handed them to us. She looked us squarely in the eyes and simply said, "They are wrong. The other reports are all wrong. I can't believe they told you this. He will certainly go to public schools."

I thank God for professionals that are confident enough in their knowledge that they will give an honest opinion no matter what the other experts in their profession are saying. I wanted to jump up and shout, **"Hallelujah!"** Instead, we continued to explain all the events of our past weeks.

Dr. Hitner finally said, "Look, if it will make you feel better, I can take pictures and make slides of his eyes. Take them to any doctor you like and let them confirm this." We said we'd like to have the slides.

It may seem odd that our reaction to her news was so negative at first, because of all the prayer we had been engaged in. Because her report differed so dramatically from the five other doctors, it took a while for this to sink in.

Dr. Hitner explained that Matt did have some eye problems:

his vision was probably about 20/200. His left optic nerve might be a little small but certainly developed, and **HE WAS NOT GOING TO BE BLIND!**

We could hardly contain our excitement! After we got in the car, we literally whooped and hollered and praised the Lord and acted not at all like most Baptists and Methodists act! We understood exactly how the lame man in the Bible went walking, leaping, and praising God after he was healed. We stopped to call Dorothy and Dude on the way home; and, of course, they shared our excitement.

We understood that, while the five doctors had probably been accurate in their assessments, something had changed. God had answered our prayers!

We had to make a lot of phone calls, as many people all over the state had been praying. Most people shared our joy, but, of course, the voice of the skeptics can always be heard at times like this. We just didn't worry about them. This was our story. The experience had happened to us.

Our God had heard us and had done the impossible to man.

Our God had done what He said He came to do in Luke 4:18:

"...proclaim freedom for the prisoners and recovery of sight for the blind..."

Leonard Ravenhill and other pastors throughout the years have said that, "A man with an experience is never at the mercy of a man with an argument." While this is not always theologically true, in our case, we felt this to be true.

This changed all our family in several ways. First, we grew

closer as a family to each other and to the Lord. One might find us at any time reading the Bible together, pointing out to each other some new truth we had discovered.

Also, when the living God manifested Himself to us in a real way, He had a profound effect on our individual spiritual walks with Him. Finally, when we experience the power of God, we feel compelled to share what we know.

Our testimony offers a magnificent tribute to the Lord. Many people prayed, encouraged, and shared in the building of our faith, but, all the glory belongs to God. He is the rewarder of those who believe that He exists and seek Him with all their hearts. Ultimately, it is the grace and graciousness of God that we see answers to our prayers! No man can boast because it is not about man's work. It is all about the Lord's work!

We did take the slides of Matt's eyes to a local doctor in Huntsville who confirmed the good report about the optic nerve. We also went back to the doctor who had said the day before that Matt was blind. This doctor seemed nervous about his diagnosis and prognosis being challenged because he believed he was right.

In all fairness to him, he probably was right the day we saw him, and it was too much to ask him to change his diagnosis overnight. His final words declared, "Well, when the child is older, we will see who is right."

Each time Matt has gone back to the doctor, his diagnosis reveals a positive change. On our first return a year later, his vision was estimated at about 20/100. The main problem the doctor believed was that Matt probably would never have a driver's license. The next year his vision was estimated at 20/60 or 20/70.

At eight years of age his vision was 20/70 at long range and 20/20 at close range provided he held the reading material where he wanted it. He has always gone to public schools. He has always made straight A's, and he graduated as the valedictorian of his eighth-grade class. He reads books the same print size as all other students.

His nystagmus, or involuntary eye movement

changed dramatically, though he does still have a staccato movement in his eyes. His has been a continual, progressive healing. He can see minute objects on the floor; he can read phone numbers out of large city phone books. He can read from the very small children's Bibles which would challenge most adults' visual acuity. He scored in the top 98th percentile on his achievement tests in the first grade.

This is truly a miracle, and we thank God for this testimony!

CHAPTER FIVE
God offers hope to the hopeless!

What happens to a parent when an authority gives a prognosis of "no hope" for his/her child? Hopeless situations exist all around us. Most of us know of hopeless individuals in our communities. When a parent is told that there is no hope, the feeling of fear, depression, and finally despair begin to take over. Those words have a powerful impact on parents' lives. The method a parent uses to cope with those words will influence the entire family for the rest of their lives.

The Bible reveals countless, "hopeless" situations. Moses, approaching the Red Sea, saw "no hope" as far as the natural man was concerned, but a supernatural God transcended the natural. He provided a way for Moses to cross the Red Sea that man could not provide.

Another man pathetically void of hope was Job. He lost all his family, wealth, and health; his wife's answer was "...curse God and die." Job, on the other hand, still hoped in God; and his hope did not disappoint him. Instead, God restored all Job possessed and more.

Also, we know about the shepherd boy named, David. He faced a hopeless situation when he came up against a mighty giant, Goliath. In the natural, a boy with a slingshot and a few pebbles could not kill a giant with armor on; but, God possessed supernatural plans for the young boy, David.

Finally, Jesus, as far as the natural eye could see, was crucified, dead, and buried, but God raised Him up and He triumphed over that "hopeless" situation so that we could also triumph over hopeless situations in our lives!

In Psalm 146:5, David tells us that:

"Blessed is he whose help is the God of Jacob, who hope is in the Lord his God..."

In Romans 4:18-21, Paul says of Abraham:

"Against all hope, Abraham in hope believed and so became the father of many nations, just as it had been said to him, 'So shall your offspring be.' Without weakening in his faith, he faced

the fact that his body was as good as dead-since he was about a hundred years old-and that Sarah's womb was also dead. Yet he did not waver through un-belief regarding the promise of God but was strengthened in his faith and gave glory to God, being fully persuaded that God had the power to do what he had promised."

Psalm 42:11 provides a beautiful command that we can give to our souls in hopeless situations.

"Why are you downcast, O my soul? Why so disturbed within

me? Put your hope in God, for I will yet praise him, my Savior and my God."

For a person who accepts at face value what he sees, hears, tastes, touches, and smells as reality, then hope in God may be a struggle in the beginning. We are very much creatures of our natural senses, and beyond the live senses we become skeptical. However, the message of the Bible from Genesis to Revelation confronts our skepticism loudly and clearly.

Another dimension of reality presents itself. When we are "born again" by the Spirit of God, we enter the realm of the Spirit which goes beyond the natural and physical dimension of life. Sometimes we tiptoe because we are frightened or disquieted by this challenge to our physically-oriented lives.

God is a Spirit. Learning and moving in that realm requires a giant step of faith. However, when the physical, natural world, offers no hope or answers for us, our calculated, analyze everything world, becomes meaningless to us. Some will then begin to look to faith to provide those answers.

To the person facing a hopeless situation but willing to hope and trust in God, the rest of this book is designed to share what we learned and the steps we took that enabled us to see the hand of God move in our lives.

It is not my intention to pass out a "formula" because God is sovereign and deals with each person in unique ways. God cannot be reduced to a formula.

My desire is that what we learned, the scriptures we discovered, the experiences we had, might build up and encourage others to take a journey of faith.

Faith in the Lord is never without result, and we are never ashamed when we put our faith and hope and trust in Him. God has so many delightful little experiences just waiting for us. He waits for a nod from us to begin!

CHAPTER SIX
The parents' perspective.

Kathy and Dennis had overwhelming encouragement and support for their journey of faith. People from all over the country prayed for them, which offered great comfort in the midst of a sometimes-difficult road. People would send books, pamphlets, and cards that were sources of great encouragement.

They heard from people they didn't even know, but they had heard Matt's story, and were praying!

On the other hand, a small number of people offered words that discouraged their faith as they presented reasons as to why this happened to Matt; or their counsel was to "protect" them from the certain disappointment they felt Kathy and Dennis would encounter.

One such person came to see them while Kathy's dad, Dude, was visiting. This person proceeded to let them know it was because of sin in their lives that Matt had been born this way! Although, difficult to hear, Kathy and Dude kept quiet and didn't react to the hurtful remarks.

The visitor left, and Dude, who is not one to sit quiet in the face of wrongdoing, said he was glad that person was gone because he was either going to ask them to leave or hit them! Small miracles taking place all around them! Dude had a very strong faith and he loved his family above all else. He often came to just be with his kids during the difficult days, and it is better not to "mess" with his kids! He wanted none of that nonsense.

Sometime later that same person had a family member who

faced an equally devastating diagnosis and prognosis. Perhaps the person rethought the idea that the problem was due to the sin in their family.

Dennis owned a lumber company and many people were in and out during a day. He often asked the people who came in to pray for his son. At times, he would feel a wall go up when he talked about trusting God for Matt's healing. When you are the one standing in the need of prayer, you can feel the support or lack thereof, even when there are no words spoken.

One lady, though, told Dennis she would NOT pray for Matt to be healed. She had been listening to an evangelist and she wanted nothing to do with that healing business! However, a few days later, she came back and said that she had been praying about this, and God told her that she SHOULD be praying for this baby and his healing. She was sincerely sorry for her initial reaction, and humbly admitted she was wrong. She said that she would certainly be praying for little Matt. The next Sunday, she was in the choir and the congregation was singing,

"Victory in Jesus." When they sang the part about, "...how he made the lame to walk again and caused the blind to see..." she locked eyes with Dennis and had the biggest smile on her face.

From that day forward, she faithfully prayed for Matt and lived up to her reputation as a strong prayer warrior. She often inquired about Matt and genuinely cared about him throughout his whole life.

The negative reactions are sometimes due to fear that nothing will happen, and there might be terrible disappointment.

Sometimes they are just unbelief. Whatever the reason, when confronted with whether we can believe God for a miracle, we are challenged to think and seek God. That's a good thing!

One last incident happened when Dennis was not home, and Kathy was by herself. A person came to her home and wanted to tell Kathy that they were going down a path that would lead to certain disappointment. They believed the medical facts should be accepted; the best path for everyone was to just accept the inevitable and move on with their lives.

Although the naysayers showed up and were a part of real life, the vast majority of people were supportive, encouraging, and praying. Their support provided the framework for our family to continue to seek God for whatever He had for them!

CHAPTER SEVEN
Consumed by the Word of God!

It is important to find out what God wants for each individual circumstance.

I cannot make a blanket statement that God will heal everyone who asks. Our job is to seek God for our needs and accept the methods He wants to use to meet those needs.

As we study His Word concerning our situations, He begins to speak to us about what He wants. We can trust Him to give us His highest and best. In the beginning of this trial, I knew that God desired to heal Matt. Sometimes the Lord just gives us that knowledge at the onset. Other times His will is revealed slowly, as we seek Him. We began to study, meditate, and discuss the following scriptures. They became our constant companions.

Psalm 103:1-4
Psalm 107:15-22
Psalm 138:1
Proverbs 9:5-8
Proverbs 4:20-22
Isaiah 44:24-25
Isaiah 53:4-5
Matthew 4:23-24
Matthew 3:16-17
Matthew 10:1
Matthew 11:3-6
Matthew 11:28-30

The burden may be too heavy to you, but not to Jesus.

>Matthew 17:20
>Matthew 18:19-20
>Matthew 19:20
>Matthew 20:29-34
>Matthew 21:21-22
>Mark 6:12-13
>Mark 8:22-25
>Mark 11:23-24
>Mark 16:15-18

The great commission was for believers to go and preach the gospel. The signs that should follow believers are interesting. One is the laying of hands on the sick that they might recover.

Luke 4:40: *"...the people brought to Jesus all who had various kinds of sickness, and laying his hands on each one, he healed them."*

Luke 10:19: *"I have given you authority to trample on snakes and scorpions and to overcome all the power of the enemy; nothing will harm you."*

> John 9:1-41
> John 14:3-14
> Romans 8:28

Keep this always before you!

Romans 10:17: *"Consequently, faith comes from hearing the message, and the message is heard through the word of Christ."*

Read it, meditate, digest, believe!

> Philippians 4:6-9
> Philippians 4:19
> Hebrews 13:7-8

Jesus is always the same.

> James 5:13-16
> Peter 2:24
> 2 John 2

The following are scriptures where blindness was healed:

Matthew 9:27
Matthew 12:22
Matthew 20:30
Matthew 21:14
Mark 8:22
Mark 10:46
Luke 7:21

These scriptures began to root and grow in our hearts, and faith in our Lord increased. The next step we took was to pray and enlist the prayer support of anyone we knew who believed in the power of God. We had people all over the state and nation praying for a little guy by the name of Matt, whom many had never seen.

The last step we took was to avail ourselves of all the tapes, books, television programs, and people who could encourage us and share with us what they knew of the healing power of God. All of these "tools" of God, blessed us!

They helped us meet discouragement head on. They turned our eyes and ears away from doubt and centered them squarely on the power of God, an awesome power. The scripture tells us that God is no respecter of persons in Acts 10:34.

Although He works in different ways with different people, we are all still His children. We are special to Him. Not one of us deserves His mercy and grace, but He won't withhold them from anyone. He longs to be a Father to His children. He longs to be our Father if we let Him. He longed to be Matt's Father, and He proved this in that truly as God's child He took care of Matt as only our heavenly Father could. Matt knows that the Lord healed him as an infant and will unashamedly tell you so.

One of his earlier doctors mockingly said that he would never be a micro- surgeon. That remains to be seen, but the truth is that Matt will be whatever God wants him to be - even a micro-surgeon.

My prayer for you is that you might find the Lord in your circumstances, no matter how hopeless, as we did. I pray that you will let Him be your Father. I pray that you will put your hand in His hand and let Him lead you, reveal Himself to you, bless you, and glorify His name through you.

To God be the Glory!

POSTSCRIPT
By Matthew Gilbert

I've heard stories of miracles, angels, and God's love all my life. I've both heard and read this story many times over my 37 years. But this story is different. It's my story. Each time I read it, I marvel at the mercy and grace that God showed my family and me. I am moved by the steadfastness of those in prayer around my family during this time.

Occasionally, I get to hear this story from the perspective of different friends and relatives, and I know that "my story" has blessed them. I pray it brings the same peace and hope to you.

I most certainly do not believe that living with a disability is a curse or slight from God. I believe that Satan is alive and well in this world, and he uses every opportunity possible to sway the faith of God's children. This is our test. I've been involved with the Muscular Dystrophy Association as a summer camp counselor, and I witness child abuse and neglect every day. Even through those children, God demonstrates his power through their love and resilience.

What I must take from my story is that God is my Father and my Friend. As a sinner, even at birth, I deserved what Satan forced upon me. I deserved blindness because I am not without fault and not outside of Satan's grasp. Scripture teaches us that "all have sinned and fall short of the glory of God." But scripture also teaches that as children of the Almighty, the faithful are awarded His grace and mercy; those come in a variety of forms. I was one whom God chose to grant healing, but there is purpose in each of His gifts. Because of my story, I knew this even at the early age of six, I gave my life to Jesus Christ.

God also granted this miracle unto his faithful children who spent countless hours in prayer, in His Word, and in consolation of my family. I am forever grateful to those that gave of their time to pray for me. I've heard stories of this throughout my life, and they inspire me. These messengers deserve my deepest thanks, but God deserves all the praise because I truly believe the scripture, John 9:25, "…I was blind, but now I see!"

EPILOGUE
By Kathy K. Surratt

My nephew, Matthew, burst into our family thirty-seven years ago producing both tears of joy and agony. Things are pretty much the same today. Matt has a way of bringing "life" to any dull situation!

Dull moments don't exist when Matt enters a room. His irreverence can bring delight and irritation all at the same time. Matt was born to a normal, traditional and somewhat straight-laced East Texas family. I sometimes think Matt was born to take the straight out of their lace! Nevertheless, with great joy, we welcomed Matt into our family. Little did we know the kind of journey we were about to take.

When I penned the words of this amazing story, Matt was only thirteen years old. Today he is 37. Matt finished high school and was the valedictorian of his class. His valedictory address was both humorous and challenging to his class. He went on to Baylor University and received a degree in forensic science. He received his master's degree from the University of Texas at Arlington.

He now resides in Arlington where he is a CPS Regional Director for the State of Texas. He loves his work protecting children.

He still delights our family at gatherings, sometimes embarrasses his parents, and loves to argue and harass anyone he thinks he might be able to get "under their skin."

Matt remains "God's child!" God surely has His hand on him as his name suggests.

Aunt Kathy

www.ingramcontent.com/pod-product-compliance
Lightning Source LLC
LaVergne TN
LVHW011732060526
838200LV00051B/3156